CONSERVATION OF ENDANGERED SPECIES

SAVING THE ENDANGERED GRIZZLY BEAR

JUSTINE CIOVACCO

I0811955

Britannica Educational Publishing
IN ASSOCIATION WITH
ROSEN
EDUCATIONAL SERVICES

Published in 2016 by Britannica Educational Publishing (a trademark of Encyclopædia Britannica, Inc.) in association with The Rosen Publishing Group, Inc.
29 East 21st Street, New York, NY 10010

Copyright © 2016 The Rosen Publishing Group, Inc. and Encyclopædia Britannica, Inc. Encyclopaedia Britannica, Britannica, and the Thistle logo are registered trademarks of Encyclopædia Britannica, Inc. All rights reserved.

Distributed exclusively by Rosen Publishing.
To see additional Britannica Educational Publishing titles, go to rosenpublishing.com.

First Edition
Britannica Educational Publishing
J.E. Luebering: Director, Core Reference Group
Mary Rose McCudden: Editor, Britannica Student Encyclopedia

Rosen Publishing
Tracey Baptiste: Editor
Nelson Sá: Art Director
Nicole Russo: Designer
Cindy Reiman: Photography Manager
Karen Huang: Photo Researcher

CataloginginPublication Data

Library of Congress Cataloging-in-Publication Data

Ciovacco, Justine.
Saving the endangered grizzly bear / Justine Ciovacco. — First edition.
pages cm. — (Conservation of endangered species)
Includes index.
Audience: Grades 1 to 4.
ISBN 978-1-68048-249-2 (library bound) — ISBN 978-1-5081-0054-6 (pbk.) — ISBN 978-1-6804-8307-9 (6-pack)
1. Grizzly bear—Juvenile literature. 2. Grizzly bear—Conservation—Juvenile literature. 3. Endangered species—Juvenile literature. I. Title.
QL737.C27C56 2015
599.784--dc23

2015014103

Manufactured in the United States of America

Photo Credits: Cover bobby20/Shutterstock.com; back cover, p. 1, interior pages background Galyna Andrushko/Shutterstock.com; p. 4 Mark Newman/Lonely Planet Images/Getty Images; p. 5 BGSmith/Shutterstock.com; pp. 6, 26 Wolfgang Kaehler/LightRocket/Getty Images; p. 7 James Hager/Robert Harding World Imagery/Getty Images; p. 8 Andriy Gusak/Shutterstock.com; p. 9 Don Johnston/age fotostock/Getty Images; pp. 10, 17 Eric Baccega/age fotostock/Getty Images; p. 11 John Elk III/Lonely Planet Images/Getty Images; p. 12 Barrett Hedges/National Geographic Image Collection/Getty Images; p. 13 Tier Und Naturfotografie J and C Sohns/Photographer's Choice/Getty Images; p. 14 Cephas/Wikimedia Commons/File:Ursus arctos horribilis map.svg/CC BY-SA 3.0; p. 15 Roberta Olenick/All Canada Photos/Getty Images; p. 16 Stephen J Krasemann/All Canada Photos/Getty Images; p. 18 John E Marriott/All Canada Photos/Getty Images; p. 19 Bob Gurr/All Canada Photos/Getty Images; p. 20 Bonnie Fink/Shutterstock.com; p. 21 Arto Hakola/Shutterstock.com; p. 22 U.S. Fish and Wildlife Service, Environmental Conservation Online System, Species search result, HYPERLINK "http://ecos.fws.gov/tess_public/pub/SpeciesReport.do" http://ecos.fws.gov/tess_public/pub/SpeciesReport.do; p. 23 De Agostini Picture Library/Getty Images; p. 24 © Gabbro/Alamy; p. 25 Stock Connection/SuperStock; p. 27 © Jack Sullivan/Alamy; p. 28 Art Wolfe Stock/Cultura Limited/SuperStock; p. 29 Gary Schultz/Design Pics/First Light/Getty Images; cover and interior pages design elements murphy81/Shutterstock.com (bear silhouette), Anton Derevschuk/Shutterstock.com (fur)

CONTENTS

WHY GRIZZLY BEARS NEED OUR HELP

Grizzly bears are large brown bears that live in North America. They are powerful animals, but they still need our help. Grizzlies once lived in a large area of western North America from Alaska south to Mexico. Today, grizzlies remain in Alaska and Canada. South of Canada, less than 1,500 remain in the United States. Even fewer remain in Mexico.

A female grizzly bear, called a sow, cuddles her cubs.

Vocabulary

Endangered species are plants and animals at risk of dying out.

Grizzlies are being crowded out by people. They have less land to live on. A U.S. agency put grizzlies on a list of **endangered species** in the 1970s. The animals are considered threatened in the United States. In Mexico, however, they are endangered. In the United States, people were not allowed to hunt the bears. People also helped to save their habitat. As a result, the grizzly population grew.

Many people think grizzlies still need our help, though. The bears still face threats to their survival.

Bears have less food and shelter when people build in places where the bears live.

WHAT GRIZZLY BEARS LOOK LIKE

Grizzlies may have light tan to dark brown fur. They are called grizzly bears because their long back fur sometimes has white tips. This makes them look grizzled, or streaked with gray, in the sun.

A large adult grizzly may weigh about 900 pounds (410 kilograms) and be about 8 feet (2.5 meters) long. Adult males are heavier and larger than adult females.

Grizzlies, like this sleeping four-year-old, have long, thick back fur.

Grizzly bears can stand up on their hind legs. They

Compare and Contrast

Black bears are sometimes confused with grizzlies because they can be brown and found in some of the same areas. Why is this a problem for people counting bear populations?

often do this to see, hear, or smell better. They also may stand when attacked.

Grizzlies have large shoulder muscles and extra-long claws on their front feet to help them dig. Their claws are at least 2 inches (5 centimeters) long.

A grizzly bear is faster on four legs, but standing helps it locate food or scare other animals.

That is about the same length as the average adult human thumb!

Grizzlies can run fast on all four legs. They can move up to 30 miles (48 kilometers) an hour. Their speed helps them catch larger prey, such as goats and elk.

The grizzly's face curves in like a dish, and its big snout pokes out in front.

Grizzly claws are always sticking out, sort of like human fingers.

Think About It

Grizzlies have nails that are straight, not curved like a cat's. How might this make it harder for them to climb trees?

This helps it smell and nibble on small insects and plants in places that are hard to reach and that are not well lit.

Like human teeth, grizzlies' teeth are made to eat any kind of food. Their sharp front teeth are used to grab prey and kill it. The rest of their teeth are perfect for chewing both plants and meat.

A bear's longer front teeth are called fangs (or canine teeth), and they help it grab and tear meat.

HOW GRIZZLY BEARS SEE, HEAR, AND EAT

Grizzly bears are omnivores. That means they eat both plants and animals. They eat all sorts of animals, some as big as a young bison. They eat smaller animals, too, like fish or insects. They like to eat plants, especially berries, stems, and roots. Grizzlies hunt during the dim hours of early morning and evening.

A grizzly has tiny eyes and a big snout: which might help more with finding food?

Compare and Contrast

Grizzlies can swim, which makes it easier to catch salmon and trout. What features do fish have to help them stay away from bears?

Grizzlies' tiny eyes cannot see very well, especially when things are far away. However, grizzlies can see in full color.

Their hearing is excellent. Like dogs, they can hear high-pitched sounds. This helps them hunt small underground animals, like ground squirrels.

Grizzlies also have a great sense of smell. They can smell a human up to fourteen hours after the person has left an area.

The grizzly's sense of smell is so good that it can often sniff out insects and humans.

GRIZZLY BEAR RELATIONSHIPS

Grizzlies spend most of their time hunting for food and finding places to hide and sleep. They use their sense of smell to follow scents to find food and to stay away from other bears.

A female grizzly bear looks for food and shelter with her young cubs.

Adult males usually live alone. Females live with their cubs for about two to three years. When the cubs are old enough, they move off on their own.

Bears will move in a different direction if they smell another

Think About It

Grizzlies rub their backs against trees. This leaves their scent and hair on the tree. Why do you think they do this?

bear nearby. Male bears do not make much noise because they do not like to meet other bears.

Females communicate with cubs through woofs, snorts, and growls. A hissing noise from a cub means it is scared, and the mother will come quickly.

Grizzly bears gather only when fishing. That is because they are too busy catching fish to worry much about other bears. However, the biggest grizzlies get the best spots and the others have to settle for whatever spots are left.

A bear catches salmon traveling upstream in Alaska.

WHERE GRIZZLY BEARS LIVE

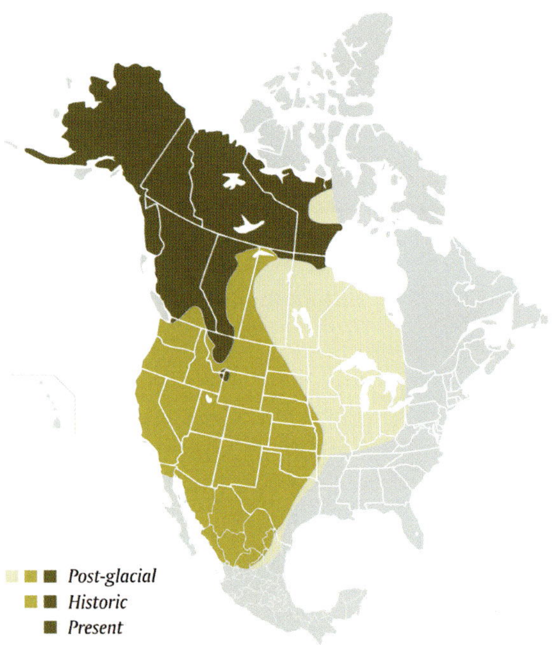

Grizzlies make their homes in and around high mountain wilderness areas. They can be found in the U.S. states of Idaho, Montana, Wyoming, Washington, and Alaska, and in parts of western Canada. Some live in thick forests, but others live on open plains. Grizzlies have even been found in parts of the **arctic tundra**.

Grizzly bears once lived in all of the shaded map areas. Today, they live only in the darkest shaded area.

Vocabulary

Arctic tundra is an area near the North Pole that is flat and has no trees. The ground there is always frozen.

Grizzlies must figure out the best area of land in which to make their home. This is called a range. Males usually have a range larger than females because they need more food. Grizzlies may walk hundreds of miles within a range to find enough food. They also try to stay away from other bears to avoid fighting for land and food. Of course, they also prefer to live away from people.

They sleep hidden near rocks or large tree roots or in caves.

This female bear found a resting spot on a small hill.

A LONG WINTER'S NAP

Late summer to early fall is a busy time for grizzlies. Adults find and eat a lot of food. They gain about 30 pounds (13.6 kg) a week. The bears are preparing to hibernate, or sleep, during the winter months.

As the air turns cooler, grizzlies look for sloped land near rocks or thick roots. They dig to make a den where they will spend the winter months. Their dens have a small opening

The inside of a den is blanketed with grasses, pine needles, and shredded branches.

Think About It

Most bears dig or find a new den each year. What would a bear do if it found another bear's den?

and a walkway to a sleeping area. The bears line the dens with dry plants that are used as beds.

Bears enter the den after the first snowfall. Mother bears live with cubs. In the den, the bears go into hibernation. During this time, they do not eat or drink, and they sleep often. To survive, a bear's body temperature drops. Its heart-beat and breathing become slower. Cubs cuddle with their mothers and sleep lightly.

A mother bear keeps her cubs close after leaving a den in spring.

Bears usually leave their dens in March or April. By then they are hungry and ready to fill up on food again.

WHY LIFE IS HARD FOR GRIZZLIES

Sometimes it is hard for grizzly bears to find food and safe places to live. Two things make life harder for grizzlies: people and changes to the environment.

People are always looking for good farmland and places to live. Sometimes they find it in the grizzly bear's natural habitat. When people

A grizzly bear rubs on objects to mark where it has been. Sometimes that happens in places where people live.

Think About It

A number of organizations exist to help protect grizzly bears. What problems do you think are most important for these organizations to solve?

move into an area, they build roads and homes, knock down trees, and clear the land. As people move into a bear's range, the bear usually moves out of the area because it can no longer find the plants and animals it needs for food. Some bears will sniff around people's homes in search of food. People may feel afraid of the bears and attack them. Bears may also be attacked by hunters looking for food.

Trash from people makes a tasty takeaway meal for bears.

A bear wanders around looking for food in Yellowstone National Park.

Environmental changes that hurt grizzly bears include global warming, which involves increasing temperatures and changing rainfall patterns on Earth. Global warming affects the types and amounts of plants that grow in a grizzly bear's habitat.

Another change is happening in Yellowstone National Park. It is now harder to find one of the bears' main food sources, whitebark pine nuts. Whitebark

Compare and Contrast

Grizzly bears are protected, but mountain pine beetles are not. Why do you think this is so?

trees are dying because of attacks by mountain pine beetles that lay eggs under the trees' bark. When the beetles bore into these trees the trees begin to die.

In addition to these trees and other plants, grizzlies also hunt for meat. Hungry grizzlies may attack farm animals when they cannot find wild prey, which makes farmers more likely to kill them.

A hungry—or angry—bear has no problem chasing a wolf.

The U.S. government cares for wild animals and their lands through the U.S. Fish and Wildlife Service (USFWS). The agency studies changes in the environment that can affect plants and animals. It uses this information to identify species that are threatened or endangered. In 1975, the agency identified grizzly bears as a **threatened species**, which means one that would likely become endangered.

A plan was set up to recover the bears. It did not allow hunting, and it set aside land where the bears would

U.S. Fish & Wildlife Service

Scientific Name	Common Name	Species Group	Listing Status
Ursus arctos	Mexican grizzly bear	Mammals	Endangered
Ursus arctos horribilis	Grizzly bear	Mammals	Experimental Population, Non-Essential
Ursus arctos horribilis	Grizzly bear	Mammals	Threatened
Ursus arctos horribilis	Grizzly bear	Mammals	Under Review in the Candidate or Petition Process

Scientists keep track of grizzlies in the wild. In some places they may be threatened or endangered.

Vocabulary

Threatened species are animals that could someday become endangered.

be protected. The plan was successful. The bear population increased. In 2007, the USFWS tried to take grizzlies off its list of threatened species. However, a judge ruled that the USFWS should keep grizzlies on the list. He said the agency did not consider the loss of the whitebark trees, an important food source for grizzlies, when making its decision.

Whitebark pine trees provide bears with tasty berries and pine needles.

WHO IS HELPING THE GRIZZLIES?

The USFWS continues to study the grizzly bear population even though the bears are recovering. The agency has several ways of studying animals and their habitats to make informed decisions. Collars or other devices are put on the animals to keep track of them and to study their behavior. The agency also counts the animals, sometimes by flying over their ranges in

A park ranger watches a bear at Katmai National Park and Preserve in Alaska.

Think About It

Conservation groups work to protect animals and habitats. Some of these groups provide information to people who live near grizzlies. How does this help the bears?

airplanes. Other scientists and groups are also devoted to helping certain animals or areas.

There are a number of local and national conservation groups that help protect grizzly bears. They let the USFWS know when they believe grizzlies need more protection. Certain groups have even sued the government for not helping grizzly bears enough.

Some believe that grizzly populations are not growing as they should. Others do not approve of a plan to allow some hunting of grizzly bears.

Researchers put a radio collar on a sedated grizzly so it can be tracked as it travels.

HOW YOU CAN HELP

Tourists watch for bears and stay out of their way in Knight Inlet in British Columbia, Canada.

One of the best ways to help grizzly bears is to learn more about their lives and problems. You may do this by visiting parks like Yellowstone National Park or by finding conservation groups online. National groups include the National Wildlife Federation and Defenders of Wildlife. Smaller, local groups also have websites with information about bear populations in their area.

Think About It

Conservation groups want people to speak up and write letters to government leaders to stop projects like drilling in Bristol Bay. Why do you think writing letters is helpful?

You can help spread the word about projects that hurt the bears' habitat. For example, many people are worried about plans to drill mines in wilderness areas such as Alaska's Bristol Bay. This would hurt the bay's large salmon population and the grizzlies who eat there.

You can also "adopt" a bear by giving money to a conservation group. Donating money can help programs to protect animals.

Some groups hold protests to make people aware of dangers to animals.

THE FUTURE FOR GRIZZLY BEARS

Bears live best in a natural habitat that has plenty of food and clean water for them.

Grizzly bears are important to the many areas in which they live. Because of this, they are considered to be an "umbrella species." This means that helping them will also help many other species and their habitats.

Grizzlies were helped the most when they were put on the endangered species list in 1975. This helped their populations grow and protected

Compare and Contrast

A bear is an umbrella species, but the moth it eats is not. Why might the bear be more important to the habitat they both share?

the lands, plants, and animals they need to survive. Today, they still need protection as people and companies move onto their land and as the climate continues to change.

People can always find ways to help the amazing grizzlies. Learning about what they need is the first step to helping them survive on lands with enough space and food.

The grizzly bear, also known as the brown bear of North America, continues to need our help.

GLOSSARY

CLIMATE The average weather conditions of a particular place or region over a period of years.

CONSERVATION A careful preservation and protection of something, such as natural resources.

ENVIRONMENT The whole complex of factors (soil, climate, and living things) that make a plant or animal or ecological community survive.

GRIZZLED Sprinkled, streaked, or mixed with gray.

HABITAT The place where a plant or animal normally lives or grows.

HIBERNATION Passing the winter in a sleeping or resting state without eating or drinking.

OMNIVORE Animal that eats both plants and meat.

POPULATION A group of one or more species of organisms living in a particular area or habitat.

PREY An animal hunted or killed by another animal for food.

PROTECT To keep from harm.

SCENT Odor or smell left behind by an animal.

SNOUT A long nose or muzzle that sticks out.

SURVIVE To remain alive; continue to exist.

WILDERNESS An area in its natural state where few people live.

FOR MORE INFORMATION

Books

Carson, Mary Kaye. *Park Scientists: Gila Monsters, Geysers, and Grizzly Bears in America's Own Backyard.* New York, NY: Houghton Mifflin Harcourt, 2014.

Kolpin, Molly. *Grizzly Bears*. North Mankato, MN: Capstone Press, 2011.

Miller, Debbie S. *Grizzly Bears of Alaska: Explore the Wild World of Bears*. Seattle, WA: Little Bigfoot, 2014.

Owen, Ruth. *Dr. Bob's Amazing World of Animals: Grizzly Bears*. New York, NY: Rosen Publishing, 2012.

Smith, Lucy Sackett. *Mighty Animals: Grizzly Bears*. New York, NY: Rosen Publishing, 2010.

Websites

Because of the changing nature of Internet links, Rosen Publishing has developed an online list of websites related to the subject of this book. This site is updated regularly. Please use this link to access this list:

http://www.rosenlinks.com/CONS/Bear

INDEX